The Life and Travels of a Law Office Dog

(As Told by Pita, the Dog)

by

Joan Poulos

DORRANCE PUBLISHING CO., INC.
PITTSBURGH, PENNSYLVANIA 15222

The contents of this work including, but not limited to, the accuracy of events, people, and places depicted; opinions expressed; permission to use previously published materials included; and any advice given or actions advocated are solely the responsibility of the author, who assumes all liability for said work and indemnifies the publisher against any claims stemming from publication of the work.

All Rights Reserved
Copyright © 2009 by Joan Poulos
No part of this book may be reproduced or transmitted in any form or by any means, electronic or mechanical, including photocopying, recording, or by any information storage and retrieval system without permission in writing from the author.

ISBN: 978-1-4349-0466-9
Printed in the United States of America

First Printing

For more information or to order additional books, please contact:
Dorrance Publishing Co., Inc.
701 Smithfield Street
Pittsburgh, Pennsylvania 15222
U.S.A.
1-800-788-7654
www.dorrancebookstore.com

Thanks to my family for their tolerance of Pita's and my visits. Thanks also to my office staff, especially Teresa and Liz (and Ella), who let Pita out. Special thanks to my husband, David, for his love and good humor.

One

It was just an ordinary day in our law office. The young, pretty receptionist was forcibly reminding the waiting courier that a document had to be filed that day in the clerk's office in the courthouse fifteen miles away. He had been through this before and just smiled, shrugged, took the two-inch thick pile of documents from her, and headed out the door.

It is a good thing that she is young and energetic. She was answering the phone, filling out an intake form for an impatient client who had a wiggling child firmly by the hand, and all the time signaling me to get into the back office and go under the desk.

I took another look around the front office, sniffed at the Persian rug lying in front of the door, and glanced out of the window at the truck which had just pulled up. Since it all looked peaceful, I turned around and trotted back to my domain under the big desk in my lady's office.

Apparently there was no danger to anyone I was supposed to protect at the moment, so I curled up (never taking my eyes off the door from her office to the hall) and waited for my lady to come back.

It was one of those hot California days. When you are wearing a long black fur coat all day, with a very stylish white ruff around my neck and on my paws, heat is not my friend. I was glad the office was kept cool but wished that just once I could take off the fancy red leather collar with the dangling yellow tags and go roll in the cool grass lawn next door. I should be used to hot weather, since I am an Australian shepherd born in the hills just thirty miles from here and I have been here all my life. Still, as I tell the guys I meet in the dog park, cool is good. Although I weigh only about thirty-five pounds, have brown eyes, and no tail, I do have a lot of hair. I try to keep it pretty neat and tidy, though, and since I didn't get to roll in much, I was usually allowed inside in the hot summer.

Most people think that a law office is not a particularly exciting place to be. I doubt they have spent much time in one. It is true that some days are quiet, especially when all the lawyers are gone and it's just me and the paralegal, but when the office is full of clients it can get pretty hectic. Some people yell; some people cry. Some children are sweet and like to pat me; others pull my ears and ruffle my fur. I get nervous about big men who walk boldly into my lady's office. If I growl, she puts me outside on the patio and that can be *really* hot, even though it is shady. I hate watching the squirrels running along the fence. If I could only climb, they wouldn't think they were so smart.

Usually there is just a lot of talking and papers being passed around. Sometimes, if someone is yelling and I am in the back office, I come out into the reception area. Some people don't like dogs. Usually that feeling turns out to be mutual, but I think I have to really check out someone who is yelling. Most people are pretty nice. One lady didn't like me since I tried to lick her hand (she smelled like liver). She swatted at me. We didn't take her case. Later another lawyer called, and asked my lady if he could rent me. (He had taken her case and was sorry.)

I wasn't born in a law office. My being here is actually an accident. I wasn't bred to be in a law office. I am a sheep dog. English is not my first language. Even though I am an Australian shepherd and have always lived in the United States (both apparently English-speaking countries), I have my own language. Since I was born in the hills of Yolo, maybe it's an indigenous, pre-verbal language. I am pretty good at using it to get what I want.

The hills around the ranch where I was born in the early fall had already been dry and brown, with that early fall smell of northern California. The daytimes are very hot and dry. It's pretty remote and not at all near a law office. Sometimes you can smell a grassfire burning down along the freeway or up in the higher hills where summer fires often start. At night, there is usually a faint breeze, smelling vaguely like the ocean, since the San Francisco Bay is just over the hills and the breezes come up from the Carquinez Straits.

I barely remember my mother. I was the last of eleven pups. Everyone thought my mother had finished delivering her pups and started cleaning them. She was just struggling to finish her delivery when the lady who owned the kennel shouted that there was another puppy on the way. That was me. My welcome didn't get any warmer the whole time I was on that sheep ranch.

I was by far the smallest of the group. Since we were all purebred Australian shepherds, my siblings were eventually registered. No one bothered about me. I was black and white, like my working-dog parents, and would never be a show dog, so registration didn't seem to matter.

We were born in an outdoor kennel in the foothills above Cache Creek. In California, since the hills are green in the winter and very brown in the summer, if they have grazing rights up in the hills ranchers move the sheep up higher where it's not so hot. There aren't too many who do that anymore, and now it's mostly just to a higher pasture where the air is a little cooler and a little cleaner. Mostly those days are gone but the kennel owner who owned this ranch had a deal with a rancher who had his land under some kind of conservation easement. He didn't plow or spray so he liked the sheep to graze his land. She had to send at least three good dogs, since there weren't many fences, and the boy who went with them couldn't always find all the sheep. Usually my mother was one of the chosen, but not this year because of her pups.

I was born before the sheep came down, so my mother really wanted to get back up to the sheep. It was very hot, but the evenings were getting cooler. When you're a puppy you just want to stay warm, but it's hard if you get too hot. We panted a lot and burrowed into the straw bedding. My mother kept walking to the edge of the fence of the kennel, looking for the sheep.

She would pace up and down, trying to see her herd. Australian shepherds depend on their eyesight, which is very keen. Sometimes she would see some sheep high on the hill and would whine sadly. She wanted to go. Herding sheep was her job, not raising puppies.

She did take care of us though she didn't have much patience with so many puppies. Since I usually got crowded out, I would follow my mother to the fence where she was keeping watch, hoping I could get her to let me eat. She usually snapped at me and walked along the fence, up and back, up and back. Maybe this first introduction to fences, which made my mother so unhappy, is why I hate fences—all fences—to this day. They keep you from doing your job.

I kept trying to eat. I refused to give up. I couldn't push my brothers away, but I was very quick and sometimes could squeeze in before my sisters got started. My sisters weren't as big as my brothers, but they were a whole lot sneakier. Even though I was one of them, they didn't want to share. When I pushed and pushed to get in, they would bite my mom just as I got there to nurse. She would whirl, growl, and get up. I guess being a nursing mother isn't too much fun anyway and surely not when someone bites.

Sometimes I was just too late. My mother would snap at me and push me away. She had finished before I started. I learned to be very fast, and I still eat that way. I was hungry lots of times, but I would sometimes get there first and get a few mouthfuls before my brothers fully woke up. I learned to sleep very lightly. I would wake up and see my mother looking out at the hills, growling if she saw a coyote up on the edge of the ranch. But she couldn't get out. I felt sad that she was so unhappy. Now I know what it is like to have a job to do and not be able to do it.

My mother and father were both working sheep dogs. I never saw my father, but he apparently loved to work sheep. I know my mother did. She worked with the sheep the kennel owner had as well as with other herds. Even though she was a registered Australian shepherd, (as was my father and several of my littermates were marked like other Aussies—Merle, and several had one blue eye), my mother was brown eyed and marked like a Border collie. I look like my mother—like a working dog, not a show dog. This always confuses people, even now when I live in town. I get stopped when we walk in the greenbelt and people ask whether I am a Border collie. People apparently think I am some kind of freak collie, since I am smaller by half and have no tail. My lady assures each inquirer that I am an Australian shepherd and that, no, I won't develop eyes of different colors or grow a tail.

She assures me that she really prefers brown eyes, so I just lick her hand to show that I haven't developed some kind of complex about how I look.

Two

My first days were touchy. My mother had so many other pups that she had little time (or milk) for me. The kennel owner was a nice lady, but she had lots of problems with the county (who thought she had too many dogs) and neighbors who agreed. She had worked at the University and had developed a working relationship with the veterinary school to breed dogs with a genetic problem. The University was trying to understand why some disorders appeared in some dogs in the same litter and not in others. Her work wasn't very popular with many people, and she was stopping, even though she had spent many years trying to develop the genetic pattern that they wanted to study. She was determined to improve the predictability of the health of working dogs. Enough people were working on show dogs, she thought, but she was always somewhat of a contrarian. So is my lady, luckily for me.

Since no one anticipated me, I was the odd dog out. My mother wasn't part of any study. She was a working dog, and many ranchers wanted her puppies. I was so little and likely not to survive, so no one spoke for me. Three of my brothers went to Colorado, where I guess they get to herd sheep, and two sisters were apparently sent to Montana, where they are having pups who turn into working dogs for the ranchers there. I think I am the only one who gets to live in an office or by the ocean. But I do miss being around sheep. I think herding lawyers must be harder than herding sheep, but it is my life. (I'm sure lawyers talk more.)

Three

Sadly, just before I was born, the kennel owner found out that she was dying She had only a few months to live. She had started giving away dogs and placing her best dogs with breeders who would continue the working dog line she was so proud of. I wasn't on anybody's list. She didn't know what to do with me. She knew all too well what happened to dogs that nobody wanted, and she was determined to find me a home.

When I was very young, I started drinking milk out of a saucer since my mother had too many puppies. I was pretty sure I was going to make it even though I was hungry a lot. None of the breeders wanted me since I was so small, and the kennel owner couldn't talk her heir into keeping me. She had a lot on her mind and details to work out. So one day she loaded me into her truck and took me with her to her lawyer. That was my first trip to a law office.

I was very scared to be in that big moving box. I had seen the truck but had no idea what it was. Since I had never been inside anything but the kennel, I whimpered in fear. That was the first of the many rides I was to have in a truck, but now I mostly ride in a Dodge Ram with a timber-rack and not the old, rundown pickup I started in.

I had never seen a town. There were so many cars on the road. It was so noisy, and there were bad smells, like cars made on the ranch. I missed the quiet of the ranch but I could sense that the kennel owner felt as if this was my only chance. I made up my mind to be strong. I only cried a little, but mostly when the kennel owner (her name was Iris, but we never heard anyone call her that) did.

She came out to the kennel with a cardboard box with a rag in the bottom. She tenderly put me in, but I was very scared and tried to claw my way out. She pushed me down and closed the lid. I started howling and pushed the box open. She seemed to understand and opened the box, and I huddled in the corner, still scared but at least the box was open.

She put my smaller box into the big box on wheels, which I now know is a truck, and we started down the road. I couldn't see much over the sides of the box and was tumbled from side to side. First there was the dust of our road, then a noisy road with little stones flying all around, then a very fast trip on a road with other trucks and lots of noise and fumes. I tried to hide under the rag in the box, but it didn't work. I started growing up, right then. Iris had a little machine she talked into. She called someone she said was her "lawyer" and said she was coming in for an appointment. She said it was important. Later I found out why she was in such a hurry.

Iris and her lawyer had been friends for many years, and the kennel owner thought she could convince her friend to take me. Everything was set except that the office didn't contact the lawyer. When we arrived at her office, she wasn't there. They said she was in court.

I never yet have been there, but it must be pretty important, since the women in the office seemed shocked that the kennel owner would expect to see a lawyer who was in court.

This was my introduction to a law office. I was brought in from the truck (where I was very afraid, since I had never been outside the kennel before) and placed on a hard, wooden floor. I tried not to pee on their floors, but I was really scared. I peed. I couldn't walk. My legs went out from under me, and the girls who were watching me all laughed. I couldn't see what was so funny but they were nice to me. One of them said they had a stuck-up client they would let hold me and maybe I could pee all over her expensive dress. I had no idea why they were all laughing so hard at the idea.

Since the lawyer wasn't there, the girls in the office couldn't keep me. They gave me some water in a little bowl I still use (apparently it is odd for a dog to have a cut-glass drinking dish) but I was so afraid I couldn't drink. I crouched down as little as I could so that they wouldn't see me and put me back into that truck, but they found me. I was so afraid that I wet all over them and made them laugh even more. I was very frightened, but their laughter didn't seem cruel. Iris seemed sad, but she was the kind of woman who did not give up easily. She said we would be back. I learned later that she was one who always kept her word.

We started back to the ranch. This time I knew what the truck was and wasn't so scared. Everything was still so strange. When I got back to my mother, I found there was only one other puppy left. There was no fresh straw, and I knew things had really changed.

My mother was nervous and jumpy. She snapped at me and pushed me away when I tried to nurse. I think I smelled like the truck, and the truck had taken away her puppies.

I didn't know what to do. She wanted to be up in the hills, working.

I tried to hide. I found a bale of hay in the corner of the barn and crawled under it.

It was warm and smelled sweet, like new hay. I went to sleep. I was hungry, but my mother pushed me away when I tried to nurse. That was the last time I ever saw her.

I slept a long time. Finally the kennel owner came out, gave me some milk, and said something about another trip tomorrow. I was too tired to worry. I did, for the first time, try some of the dry, tasteless chips she offered me. I would not take them from her hand, but when she put them into the dish where my mother always ate, I tried them.

That night I slept in the hay bale—all alone. I remember how lonely I felt. I still don't like to be alone, unless I have a job to do. I tried some more of the tasteless chips. I didn't much like them, but I was very hungry.

The next day the workers who had come to clean the kennel coaxed me out with a saucer of milk, grabbed me, and put me into the truck again. I was on the way to my first bath.

Apparently the girls at the law office didn't like the way I smelled. I thought the sheep smell was wonderful and just because the hay I slept in had been used by the sheep before they put it into the kennel was no problem for me. I liked to smell like my mother and the sheep she loved so much. It made me feel like I belonged somewhere.

When the truck stopped this time, I was taken out and put into a very small wire cage.

I cried. The people in the shop were busy washing dogs, combing out coats and cutting toenails. I didn't want any part of it. I crawled into the far back corner and tried to hide under the little mat in the cage. It didn't work. It was eventually my turn. I was taken out, patted, and reassured that wouldn't hurt. I did not like it. I still don't even these many years later though it is a regular part of my life.

I was bathed, clipped, and given something that made me poop. They said I had worms, but I don't see how that could be. I don't even know what a worm is, and I surely didn't get it in the milk. They started giving me some more of the dry crunchy food. I was hungry, but this still didn't taste very good. The ultimate indignity was that when they finished blowing dry my fur, they put a ribbon around my neck.

A working sheep dog doesn't take kindly to a red ribbon around the neck. I tried to get it off, but they kept putting it back on while they drove me again to the law office—this time in a wire cage. I tried but I couldn't bite through that ribbon. I quieted when I recognized the parking lot.

In a funny kind of way, I was glad to be there. I knew I wouldn't be hurt. People seemed busy and moved quickly but no one was mean to me. When they took me out of the truck, I was glad to be out of the wire cage and in a bigger place.

I had never been inside a house before I was there the other day, but I did understand that humans liked big spaces and I might be lucky enough to live with a human in a warm, safe space. I had seen my mother go into the kennel owner's place, and she always seemed happy when she came back. I wished I had been taken in too. I always got left outside.

The lawyer was in the office this time. She was busy and rushing around. She was different from the kennel owner and had things on her feet that made noise when she walked.

I cowered on the floor. I tried to crawl under the big wooden box and hide. Iris wouldn't let me. When I licked her hand, she smiled but seemed very sad. She told me this was my best chance and I should behave. I just scrunched down. It was nice in the corner under the big box (I know now it is called a desk and consider it my den.)

The lawyer, who was pretty tall and younger than Iris, rushed into the room saying she didn't have time for a dog. She said she wanted to help but she didn't think this was going to work. That's the first time I really knew they were trying to leave me there. She patted Iris on the back and said she would help anyway she could, but she was just too busy to have a puppy.

Iris didn't cry but bit her lip. She was trying so hard to get good homes for her dogs before the cancer got her. The way they said that word, I could tell it was something bad. I could tell she was trying to be brave. I felt bad, but I also was really worried about what was going to happen to me.

I crawled carefully toward the lawyer. I was born with no tail, but I wagged what I had.

The lawyer crouched down and touched my head with her finger.

I saw that she had brown eyes like my mother and like mine, and I wanted to smell her. I put my head down and looked at her. I wagged my tail so hard I almost peed again. That wouldn't have been very smart. I just kissed her finger. It seemed to please her because she smiled at me. She had light colored hair, sort of like the straw in my kennel. Her face was soft and friendly. When she picked me up and stood up, I snuggled under her hair. She didn't smell like anything I knew. She didn't smell nearly as good as the sheep next door, but a little like the flowers around our kennel. I licked her neck. I felt like I would be safe. I was afraid to hope. It was sort of like getting my sisters away from mother so I could nurse and then having her move. I took a chance and really, really started hoping I could live with this woman. I decided she was my lady. I was in love.

The good news for me was that she was too. I was her dog from that minute. She held me and patted me, as she told Iris goodbye. She asked about my food and was given some of the awful dry food they used in the kennel. She rubbed her cheek against my fur, and I kissed her hand. I think we bonded in ten seconds. I know that from that minute on, wherever she is, I want to be there. I never thought about my mother or the kennel again. It made me sad when she cried as she said goodbye to Iris. I think Iris must have been a really nice person, even though I really didn't get to know her. She seemed happy that another of her dogs had a home. I found out later that she died a couple of weeks later. I was lucky; I had a new home—in a law office.

My new home seemed so big. My new lady (I don't call her my owner since I think I own her just as much as she owns me, and titles don't seem to fit) understood. She put a jacket (hers) down on the floor by her feet and put me under her desk. She offered me a treat, but I had been trained to eat only from the bowl at the kennel and never did get used to taking food from anyone's hand. I crawled between her feet and went to sleep on the jacket. I had found my den.

Even though I am now a big dog and know how to tell her when I have to go outside or when she should listen to me about the person coming into the office, I still love my den. It is under an antique desk. The desk is big with a marble top. It has drawers, and I heard that it used to belong to a governor of California. I am not sure what that is, but I guess I'm supposed to be impressed. They call it a desk, but it is my den.

I know when I am there I feel safe. Sometimes I stay there while my lady goes to court. Sometimes I stay there when she does something she calls "taking depositions."

I don't care because I know she will always come back, and I will keep that office safe until she does. This is my job, and I never feel lonely when I am working. I do know how my mother felt about the fence though. If I am shut away from my lady, I don't like it. It is my job to keep her safe, and I don't want to be interfered with.

When it was time to leave, I was scared. I had grown used to the office and the safe, dark place under the desk. I had met the secretaries (that is what they call the women I had met the first time I was there), and they were told to take care of me. My lady took me outside and told me to go pee. I had no idea what she was talking about, but I really had to relieve myself. I squatted and apparently did the right thing because she patted me and praised me. I was surprised since I was just making myself feel better but I was glad it pleased her. To this day when she points and says, "Go pee," I try, even if I don't really have to.

That's what I mean about English. I really don't understand some things. Like when she wants me to sit before I jump out of the back seat of the car, she says, "Sit." Sometimes she says, "Sit down," or sometimes she says, "You know what you are supposed to do." Apparently they all mean the same thing but I really get confused. Sometimes I just stand there and look at her and she gets annoyed and yells, "Sit!" I would like to ask her why she didn't just say that in the first place.

It was almost dark out when I was put into a truck again and moved to another place. This truck was different. It didn't have the nice sheep smells or the hay in the seat. The seats were leather so I liked the smell of them, but the vehicle was very different. This was a car. I was to see a lot of them in the future, but this day I was really scared. I started whimpering.

Although she had put me into a back seat with her jacket, my lady stopped the car and put the jacket and me into the front seat with her. That was one of the only times I had ever ridden in the front seat but it made me feel better. I crawled over and put my head into her lap as we drove, and I was contented. I didn't care where we were going; my home was and is with her.

Five

When we got to where we were going, I was lifted from the car. I was afraid. My lady, once again, put me on her shoulder and against her neck, and I hid under her hair. That was wonderful. We walked into another building, this one even bigger than the office.

There was a man there. He was so big and so tall I was afraid. I ran to my lady, and she picked me up. She introduced me to David and told me he would take care of me too. He does, and he and I spend a lot of time together. However, the first time I saw him, he seemed so big, and I was scared!

I didn't know what to think. The man held me. He smelled good. He had a lot of hair (humans call it a beard), and I liked it when he snuggled me against his neck like my lady had done. He is now my second favorite human. He has a nice low voice, and he takes care of me.

He pets me and scratches my butt, which my lady doesn't do. He is wonderful and better than anyone is, except my lady. I try to take care of him too, but I always focus on her. It is my job to take care of her, and I try my best.

Then a little people came in. She was really small and wanted to hold me. I was scared.

My lady held me and let the little girl pet me. "The child" (that's what they call the little people) asked what my name was.

I hadn't any name. The kennel didn't name its puppies. My papers just said "Puppy, Kennel, etc." My lady had just called me Puppy. It didn't really matter to me, because I didn't really understand anyway. But this child, who they called Kady, said they couldn't just call me Puppy. She said since I was so tiny they should at least call me a "Puppita." That became my name.

Since no one bothered to register me, this was my naming ceremony. Puppita soon became Pita, and that is my name now. Lots of people say it sounds like bread, but I don't care. It is my name, and it is a whole lot nicer than what the kennel workers used to call me when I crawled under their feet when they raked out the straw.

I was put down on the floor to explore. I was on the same kind of wood floor they had in the law office but this one had even more coverings. They are apparently called rugs. I walked around and had to pee. I chose one very soft one to pee on and caused quite a commotion.

It seemed okay to me. It was in a corner and the goofy flower pattern seemed like I was out in a field. I guess that was a mistake.

They started yelling, lifted me, and ran outside yelling, "No!" They started wiping and trying to get up the spot. Apparently I had picked a very expensive rug they called a Persian for my field of relief. I didn't understand. I was put outside by a huge puddle of water (they call it a swimming pool), and I was very frightened. They were talking in loud voices and seemed upset. To this day, one rug looks the same to me as any other, Persian or not. I just try never to get where I can't convince someone to let me out when I have to pee.

My lady saw that I was scared, so she came out, picked me up, and put me against her neck. Then everything was okay. I soon learned that I wasn't to pee on that rug. Even though it turned out to be a very expensive oriental rug, it is still my favorite place to sleep (other than my big round pillow bed), but that is okay, I guess.

That first night I was hungry. They gave me milk but I didn't really want it. They gave me bits of hamburger, which I still love, and some dry dog food. It wasn't very tasty—it was the food the kennel used and had little taste. Not until the next day did we agree on my food. To this day I get a can of canned dog food (lamb and rice) and unlimited dry food (much better quality than the kennel had). Most recently, the lady has taken to giving me the bones and extra meat when she cooks, and I really like that. I especially like the bones from spare ribs but she isn't too happy when I throw them up on yet another expensive rug. Humans get so upset when you pee or barf! They have a weird sense of what really matters.

The first night at the lady's house, I cried during the night. They had bought a kennel for me. I hated it. They put me into the crate and shut the door. I cried. They opened the door. I still cried. Finally they put me on a pad outside the kennel, and I went to sleep and slept until early morning. I still have to wake them up so I can go out, but as they are getting older they sleep more but fortunately I do too.

Those first few nights were tough. I didn't like peeing in my kennel, but I couldn't wait. They cleaned it out and put me back. I cried. I outlasted them. I tried to bite through the door. I tore up the blanket they put in for me to sleep on. I hated it. It was even worse than the fence that had kept my mother in.

They didn't understand that I couldn't stand being in a cage. The first few times we traveled, they took the kennel. I cried and cried until they opened it up. I am quiet and content if they just take my bed, but the cage is a prison to me. It was really bad when they took me for some shots, and the vet had to give me anesthesia and do some surgery. I wasn't away from my lady long and they were pretty nice to me in the hospital, but I was really upset. Unfortunately that became my vet, and whenever he comes to our house to give me a shot, I try to bite him. I wouldn't really hurt him, but I don't want him to come back. My lady holds my mouth shut and keeps me from moving, but it's hard for me to see why she lets him stick me with a needle.

Six

My life became a little more routine. No matter how tough the nights, the days were fine. I got to go to the law office. Soon I understood that people would come into my lady's office, and I was not supposed to growl. Since I weighed about fifteen pounds, nobody was really afraid of me, but my lady was very firm that I was not to do this.

I would walk up to her visitors and see how they smelled. If they were afraid of me, I would not be very happy but would just go back into my den. The only time I got really upset was when one man smelled funny. I didn't like him, and I kept nudging my lady, trying to move her away to a safe place. She just kept patting me, under the desk, not telling me to go outside or anything. He got up and started around the desk. I came out growling; he backed off.

I didn't even get scolded, so I guess my instincts were right. My lady told him to leave, and I heard her tell the receptionist not to ever make another appointment with him. She thought he was on drugs. (I guess that is bad.)

After that I was pretty much a hero to the secretaries. I got a few treats, and they didn't seem to mind as much when I wandered out to the front. I settled into the office routine and things were pretty normal. We go to the office for a few days and then we get into the car and go to the other house by the ocean. The ocean is really big—bigger even than the swimming pool I once fell into. I don't go into the water here, but there is a beach I get to run along and chase the seagulls.

Our house there is on a pretty big lot, and I get to stay outside. It's my job to keep the place safe so I chase lots of cats that people have dumped there. Sometimes I even chase the deer. Once I caught one and learned that deer can *really* kick. I won't do that again. Loud barking is enough to get them to jump out over the tall fence.

Then after a couple of days we go back to the city and the law office. It is a pretty long trip, but I have a special lining that makes me feel safe. I sleep until we get back to the office; then I can go back into my den and take over my job guarding the office and my lady.

Seven

And then my family decided to take a trip. Riding in the car is one thing, but the first time we took a really long trip together we took the truck. It is totally different from Iris's truck. I can see out of this one really well. It belongs to David and has a lot of smells like the ranch but not of sheep. Maybe I could get him to buy one to make things smell better.

Since my lady had decided she needed a vacation (I'm not sure what that means except it meant that I didn't get to go to the office for a while), I was in the truck a really long time.

It was a long trip. We went away from the law office and clear across California. The first time we stopped for lunch I was really scared. I had to pee and I was thirsty, but I didn't like the hot, dry ground. There were big mountains around, and I couldn't tell where I was. We parked by the edge of a big pond of water (they call it a lake). It's not as big as the ocean but there was no beach between it and me and I was scared.) Then my lady took her own glass of water, poured it into a saucer, and gave it to me. I drank it all. I was so thirsty but I didn't want to stand outside the truck and drink. I was afraid they would go away and leave me.

Maybe humans like this kind of place but my ears hurt and it seemed a little hard to breathe. I sure wasn't going for any long runs away from my lady. I was almost glad to be back in the truck.

It was a long, hot, dry trip. We went to a place called Nevada and stopped at a filling station. There was no grass on which to pee—not even any chips. I didn't know what to do. Then my lady took me on a leash and went around back of the noisy gas station, and we found a little patch of weeds. I was really glad to see them. I had to pee, and I just wanted something normal to pee on.

I slept a lot but could see that after we left California, it got hotter and dryer. There was really nothing to look at through the windows. When we first left home we went through high hills, even bigger than those around the ranch. They called them mountains and some had some white stuff on them. We just kept driving. I don't, to this day, understand why humans want to go away from their nice homes and friends to see other places that are desolate and dry. Maybe a vacation just means something different.

We finally ended up for the night in a town called Ely, Nevada. The motel said it was okay if I slept in the room if they had a crate for me. I hate crates. I hoped they would take me with them to go get something to eat. They put me into the crate after taking me for a long walk to find some grass. I couldn't eat. I was so scared I was shaking.

They said they were going out to eat. I didn't see why I couldn't go too. It was dark in the room, and it smelled funny. My lady knew I would be lonesome so she turned on the TV and left a light on but I was still panicked. What if they didn't come back? I would be stuck in this stupid crate alone.

When they left I tried to chew my way out of the crate. I chewed up the robe they left for me to lie on; I chewed up the water bowl. I was frantic. I howled and cried. No one came. I knew my lady wouldn't go away and leave me, but what if something had happened to her? I worked really hard to get out.

When they came back from dinner, I had chewed my way out of the crate. I couldn't get out of the room but I was waiting for them. They were very unhappy. I didn't see why. I was just trying to be free. I would never have left them. They didn't seem to understand how sad I was when they left me.

They cuddled, fed, and watered me, but it was still a long time before I could go to sleep. I curled up next to my lady's bed where I could hear her breathing. Not until she went to sleep could I finally give up and sleep.

Eight

The next day we drove all across the desert and went to another place, which they called Idaho. That was much better. There were trees and streams. The air was cooler, and there were fewer cars. It wasn't home, but I liked it.

We went to a city called Coeur d'Alene. It is by a big lake and was peaceful and calm. It didn't stay cool like the first part of Idaho, though, but I still liked it. We had a lucky find. We found a hotel called LaQuinta that allows dogs in the rooms, and I was very much happier there. There was more space in our room, and we were close to the outside door so I could get my lady to take me out when I had to go. That is important to a dog. We don't want to soil our den but sometimes we just have to go find a place to relieve ourselves. It turned out that we were lucky enough to stay in LaQuinta hotels again—and even in this exact room a year later.

The weather was hot, but the nights were cool and the room was big. My family didn't leave me alone much. They found out they could take me to outdoor restaurants, and I wouldn't have to stay back in the room in the crate. I really tried to be well behaved, since I hated being left behind. I decided I would act like I was in the office, crawl under the bench where my lady sat, and quietly wait for them to finish eating. That seemed to work. We went out to some property we apparently own, and they let me run and run. There were gophers and a big lake. I had a wonderful day. The restaurant at the lake even let them bring me on the deck and eat with them. I really tried to be good so I wouldn't ever have to go back into that crate.

It's interesting to see the different people in the places we go. Here there were lots of people with wet clothes. They smelled grassy, like the lake water. I guess they were in the lake and just came up on the deck to eat. They were mostly younger than my lady was, and some of them went out into some kind of box that floated on top of the water. They didn't seem to go anywhere, though, since many of them came back and got out of the box and back on to the deck while we were there. Most people seemed happy and no one objected to my being there where they were eating.

We stayed here a few days. It was really hot during the day, but I got to run on the property several times. I was tempted to go into the lake, but I don't really like water so I didn't. People who don't know me always try to throw sticks or something into the water and expect me to go in and get them. I just sit and look at them acting goofy. I don't retrieve things, let alone go into the water to do it. I'm not a Lab, although some of my best friends are.

The trip home was long, but it seemed nicer since now they knew that I was so scared of the crate. They just put my bed next to theirs, and I slept pretty well. I still had to go out a lot, but they seemed to understand when I woke them up by putting my muzzle into my lady's hand.

Nine

When we got back home, I was a little skittish. I started shaking every time my lady left me, even for a few hours. I kept remembering how horrible it had been in the crate that first night. I didn't want to be away from her, even for a few hours. My lady asked a person who is supposed to know how to train dogs. She was advised to give me some kind of tranquilizer, but she didn't like to give me any medicine I didn't really need. She decided I could spend more time in the office. I was thrilled. I like going to the office. Most people wouldn't think of a law office as a tranquilizer but it works for me.

As I have said, my lady's desk is a great big walnut one. She keeps treats in the bottom drawer, and if I act really good, she gives me one. I usually know how to get at least one treat a day.

I have a deal with the secretaries. If I have to go out and my lady is in court or somewhere else, I just scratch on the door and give a little yip. Both receptionists are really good to let me out.

I have been through quite a few different office staff members. The ones who are always there are Teresa and Liz. They both understand me and make sure I get let out to go pee—and that I will always come back. I like them a lot, and now that they have babies, I even like the babies.

My name was one of the first words Liz's little girl, Ella, said. Now I am working on her second baby, who is a boy. We'll see. He's a long way from talking but I have high hopes for Miles. He already knows not to pull my ears.

One day my lady left me at the big house. She shut all the gates and was sure I would stay in the backyard until she came back. Surprise. It wasn't too hard to see that if I pushed the logs into a big pile, I could crawl up them and get over the stone wall against which they were piled. I ran across the greenbelt to the very busy street. I guess I was lucky that I didn't get hit, but I am very fast and I did look. Anyway I went to the office. There was a new secretary, and she didn't know me. She called the court and had my lady paged. They asked if I was her dog. Too bad Teresa hadn't got there because they wouldn't have had to bother the court. She knows me. When Liz came, she knew too. She just opened the door and let me into my office.

My lady wasn't really upset. She was mad because I didn't stay home where she put me, but she was so glad I hadn't been hit by a car that she couldn't really act mad very long.

Ten

I have really learned to like traveling. Every weekend we go to the coast, so I am used to being in either the car or the truck for a couple of hours. One day, though, my family decided to drive to Santa Fe. That name meant nothing to me, but one morning very early, we all got up and loaded our stuff into the truck. This time they dragged the crate along again. I hadn't been in it (or any crate except when I get groomed), and I really hate it.

It was really foggy when we started across country. I sat up in the back of the truck (the back seat) and looked out. I couldn't see anything so I just went to sleep. When they stopped at the filling station (the signal for my pee stop), I thought we were going back to Idaho. The air smelled like the desert in Nevada. It wasn't though. We went across California and then into Arizona. It was a really long day, and when we got to the motel, they didn't even bother with the crate. We were all too tired to do anything but sleep. They kept talking about the desert, and I tried to see something out the windows. There wasn't much, but it was real warm. We started early the next day, and the big highway was really boring. I was glad when they told me were in the state where Santa Fe was. To me that meant we were almost there.

I actually liked New Mexico. We went to some Indian ruins and then went up to see an old settlement. There were dogs running around and little Indian kids who really know how to talk to a dog. I got to share the picnic and stayed (quietly for a change) chained to the picnic table with our food while my family went into the museum. All the people were nice to me in New Mexico. There are some places where you just feel welcome. The people there, who are called Navajo, are like that. They don't think dogs are something to be afraid of. They treat us like we are worth something.

I remember walking around Window Rock and there were lots of dogs in the backs of open pickup trucks. I wish I could ride in one of those. We stopped at lots of trading posts, but I think that is just another name for a different kind of store. I couldn't see that my lady traded anything but money for what she bought. I got a bone at one place, and I happily chewed it in the truck while they went into another trading post. It sure is a long way to Santa Fe but I was a lot happier once we got into Indian country.

Eleven

We finally got to Santa Fe. It looked like another big city to me. I wished we had just stayed in Window Rock. I was sure I wouldn't see many sheep here. Still, I was glad to be out of the car.

We got there late and stayed at another LaQuinta. This one wasn't nearly as big as the one in Coeur d' Alene but it was okay The people who work there are used to dogs and keep dog biscuits at the check-in guest for some of their four-legged guests. But I didn't like to be left there, even if they tried leaving me out of the crate. I sulked and whined. Finally they started taking me with them, warning me I might spend considerable time in the truck. It was worth the gamble.

There are a lot of cars in Santa Fe, but the city is different. I could smell the difference.

The houses smell more like the country. When we got to the house of my lady's friend, I could see why.

Our friends had a house made out of mud. They called it adobe, but it seemed like dried mud to me. I really liked it. It had thick walls and was cool. Inside I could walk around and smell all the smells of Santa Fe. They had a little dog (and little is the operative word). That little dog (a kind of miniature Boston terrier) was not even half my size. I was getting pretty big by now. I weighed about twenty pounds, and that little dog was really scared of me. I wasn't going to hurt it but its owners kept it in a crate away from where I was. One day, the dog was out and the two of us went outside and had a great time.

When the families came home and saw we were playing and didn't tear up their grass, they allowed us to be together inside the house and didn't put their dog into the crate. The only thing I didn't like was when that dog wanted my lady to hold him. I am very careful about strange dogs (and people) going near my lady. I got scolded for growling so I didn't do that again but I never took my eyes off him when he was close to my lady.

We went on lots of walks. Santa Fe has a great outdoor plaza. My lady and I sat on a bench while the others went out to breakfast. We met police ladies, firefighters, and lots of Indian ladies who were selling jewelry. When the rest of my family came back, I went with my man for a walk while my lady went shopping. She bought a dumb-looking hat with lots of little people (dolls they call them) around the edges. I think I could take it apart pretty easily, but I didn't get the chance. We all drove up to a place with horses and weird sculptures. They said dogs weren't supposed to be there, but since I was so well behaved and on the chain, they let us walk around. The ground was covered with good smelling wood slivers. I liked burying my nose in them and rolling around. I guess I wasn't supposed to do that, since the guy who seemed to be in charge came out and scolded me. I don't think my family was going to buy any of his stuff anyway, but they left right away. Those great big metal things wouldn't fit into our truck even if they did want one. I heard something about it being an outdoor art gallery, but I have tried to understand what humans call art and I give up. The big things didn't even do anything. I guess you are just supposed to look at them. I was glad to leave.

The biggest test was when we went to my lady's other friend's house. She had built a big, new house out on the edge of Santa Fe. It was so new that there was no yard. Everyone was admiring the view down over the city and watching the sun set. I couldn't see much to look at but I did discover one cat I tried to chase.

My lady's friend said I could come into the house. I was really nervous. Everyplace I looked there was some kind of vase or ceramic doll. The tables were so low that they were even with my head and were all covered with things that looked like they would break. I was very careful to walk behind my lady and not to move around much. She said I did well, and I got lots of pats. The friend was from some country far away and the humans talked about things that made no sense to me, but they were really interested. The dishes were so little. I guess that people from that land didn't eat much (although I noticed that they kept filling the little dishes up again.)

There was beef barbecue at the table on some kind of hot stove. It smelled wonderful. I didn't get any (at least not until we got back to the truck—my lady had wrapped up several pieces in her napkin for me). I was patient and *very* careful. The evening went well, but I was glad to get back to the motel where I could move around. My regular-size dish sure looked good.

The next day we went back to the mud house and had another good meal. They are really nice people. I think they used to live in California near my lady. She said she was sorry they had moved away.

Those people understood how nice it was to get a bite while everyone else was eating. I had another romp with the little dog, and then we all went for another walk. The streets were very dusty, and there was no grass. I have learned to pee on chips at the supermarket, but there weren't even those. I made do. I guess it was all right since when my family went to a bookstore they let me stay outside, chained to a chair where I could see them. They walked and walked.

They kept looking at art but I couldn't see much difference in the galleries. I was patient and just happy to be with my family. I smelled lots of different plants, and in one place I found there had been a coyote. I don't think my family knew the difference. They just thought it was another dog whose owner didn't have a plastic bag to pick up the evidence. But there is a different smell. I remembered that smell from the ranch where I was born. When the lambs were born, coyotes came right down into the homestead.

I was almost sorry to say goodbye to the family we visited. They were from a place called Lebanon, and my lady was very fond of her friend Mimi. Mimi's sister was visiting from Lebanon, and my lady cried when she said goodbye. Apparently it is a very long way to that place, and my lady was afraid she would not see her friend again. She was a very nice lady, but I think she was sick somehow. She seemed like she was hurting. I licked her hand, but I couldn't make her well. I don't like to see people sad.

Twelve

We left early in the morning. We went back through Gallup, where the trading posts were. At one place I got some dried meat. They called it jerky but I did like to chew on it. I would prefer it if they would not use so much salt, though.

I saw lots of Indians. Some folks say that we should say Native Americans, but the folks here talked a lot about Indian rugs and Indian jewelry. I think they were proud to be Indians. I think they must have understood dogs and sheep because it made me a little homesick to smell that familiar smell. The men didn't pay much attention to me, but the children all stopped and patted me. Their mothers just stood by and smiled. They seemed very nice. Many of them seemed to live somewhere like my old sheep ranch. I think they must have some sheep at their houses. I would like to go see, but I couldn't leave my family.

Before we stopped the next night, the weather changed. I had never seen weather like that. When white feather-like things started flying through the air, I was baffled. I was warm in the back seat of the truck, but it seemed like it got very cold outside. My family said it was snow. We stopped and I got out. I didn't like the way it felt on my feet. I tried to go around it, but it was everywhere. The funny thing was when I tried to bite it, there was nothing there. When I got covered with the white stuff, it just went away and I got all wet. I didn't understand but I tried to catch some of the white things in my mouth and was totally frustrated when they just disappeared.

My family thought it was funny. When I tried to chase the white things, I slipped and fell. The ground, all of a sudden, was cold and very slick. I was very glad to get back into the warm truck. My lady said we were back in Arizona, but it sure didn't look like where we had driven through before. I just remembered cactus plants with stickers and dry parking lots with no chips to pee in. This was totally different. They said this town was up in little mountains. It was called Flagstaff. I hoped we would just drive on, but my family said they were tired.

We drove all around Flagstaff trying to find a place to eat. We couldn't see the signs because of all the white stuff falling through the air. We gave up and went to another LaQuinta. I am getting to know those places, and it seems like they are familiar, even though they are different. They all make dogs feel at home though.

Our room was on the second floor and was very nice. I had lots of room to roam and the door at the end of the hall led to a stair that went right down to an area full of chips, where I could go pee. My family was hungry. They fed me all right, but they had nothing to eat. My lady decided to go out and walk to someplace to get some food. I was very worried. That white stuff was still coming down and it was very dark. She said I was to wait there with David and that she would be back. He didn't seem worried, so I tried not to be. I stood on the window ledge watching her cross the street. I couldn't see her. I didn't want to eat until I knew she was back, but it had been a long day and I ate and curled up on my bed (which they had brought in) and was dreaming of warm California when she came back. She brought food that my family shared with me. It turned out to be a very quiet, peaceful night.

When we got up the next morning, the ground was all white. The air was clear, and I was eager to go out. My family was slow to get dressed, and I was having trouble waiting. The first thing in the morning, I really have to pee. When I dashed out (with my lady in her bathrobe) I slid clear across the parking lot. It didn't show, but the cold night had left a coating of ice. My feet couldn't stop me, and I tumbled on my nose. It wasn't helping that my lady was laughing. I felt my nose tickling with the cold, and I could smell the big pine trees all around. Some people must like it, since there were lots of cars, but I couldn't wait to get into the truck and start for home.

Thirteen

When we got on the road, the storm had come back. This time little round bits of ice were coming from the sky. I was really nervous. What kind of place was this? I was glad we were going back to California. We went really slowly, and finally the ice stopped. My family called it hail, and my lady said it was nothing like they had in Kansas. Still, I was glad I didn't have to walk around in it. I don't know where Kansas is, but I think places where you don't get so cold are better, even though I have a big fur coat. Maybe if you live there your feet get tougher. Mine aren't. I would sure hate to try to herd sheep in the snow.

We drove and drove. It was another long day. Once again we watched the sun turn the sleet into little rainbows as we drove very carefully along the route home.

We tried to find a way to see our friends who had moved to Havasupi, Arizona. There was a lake there. It didn't mean much to me, but the water smelled good in that dry, dusty place. The edge of the dam was visible, but the route over wasn't. We drove on into California

The edge of Death Valley was a carpet of blooming wild flowers. My family discussed going inland to see the flowers. Scotty's Castle, wherever that is, figured largely in the conversation but the urge to get north pushed us on. It seemed a lot like the desert to me. I had just about seen enough of that, even if this was in California.

We got to Tehachapi before dark. The trains were coming and going; the air seemed fresh and balmy after Flagstaff. We found a motel that would allow me, and my family started trying to find a place to eat. The Chinese restaurant at the motel had an old grease smell. I was very afraid that they were going to leave me alone while they went out to eat. I knew they would come back, but I didn't want to leave them without me to take care of them. The motel wasn't very nice, and I could smell that other dogs hadn't been as careful as I am about waiting to go outside to pee. I am pretty proud of how well I can wait.

We walked all around the town. The Catholic Church had a lovely lawn that I visited with great glee; the sidewalks wound around the area near the highway. We walked for a long time, and then my lady said she wanted to go back. We returned to the motel, and David went to find provisions. He found a liquor store and evidently they had a good smelling store they called a delicatessen. He brought back sandwiches, olives, pickles, and all that stuff humans like. He even brought me some jerky. I wasn't really worried, since my family always has my chips and my cans of food with them. Even if they have a hard time finding somewhere to eat, I always get my meals. That's pretty important to me especially since when I started out I was never sure that I would get enough to eat.

I didn't like the many people who went in and out of this motel, but finally we all settled down to sleep. It was good to be back in California. I'm not really sure what that means, but to me it sounds closer to home.

The next day we drove north, stopping at strange outposts. It was raining, and my family likes to see different things. I mostly stayed in the truck, but at one place I went in with them and wandered around a place that had lots of smells of cats and squirrels. I didn't get to chase any of them, though, and I was glad when we got back into the truck and started going home. There is something very soothing about sleeping in the truck when it is raining.

Highway 99 isn't very interesting to a dog, or maybe to anyone, but it is better than Interstate 5. There are lots of little towns and big towns. I saw lots of empty stands where they apparently sell vegetables. I wouldn't be interested anyway, but maybe in the summer it is more interesting. I was glad to be home, but very tired.

Fourteen

I liked being back in the office. One day, everybody was very upset. There had been a burglary. Even though I spent most of my time in a law office, I didn't know what that meant. I did understand that someone had come into my office without telling us and had taken some of our stuff. I wish I had been there. I wouldn't have let them in. I sniffed around the office, but I couldn't find anything but a cigarette butt outside our door. I knew it didn't belong there because that is where I lie when there is someone in the office who doesn't like dogs. I know it wasn't there because my lady doesn't like smoking and doesn't allow it at our office. I checked her bottom drawer, and my treats were still there. I can't figure out why she is so upset about someone getting into her files. Apparently whoever came in took our friend's computer and his files and our computers from the front office but overlooked the main computer in the center office. It was a real jumble in there, and that was where the main computer was that had all the files in it. I don't really understand anything about this but I know my lady was pretty upset. They took something that had belonged to her mother—some stock, she said. I thought stock was cattle or sheep, but apparently to lawyers it's something different. I have to learn a whole new language here. I listen, but the words don't always mean much to me. I've heard some clients say the same thing.

Pretty soon things went back to normal. I had some shots. Just when I am getting relaxed at the coast and thinking all I have to do is roam around chasing cats (who live in the dunes)—and something I think looks like a cat but it squirts something horrible (they call it a skunk)—the doctor who lives down the street comes to call. I don't mind him, but he always brings a shot for me. I don't like that. I try to bark especially hard when I hear him coming but it doesn't seem to scare him away.

I really like routine. I like to sleep in my bed next to my lady's bed, especially when she's home and in it. I don't really care whether we are in Davis, where my office is, or at the coast, where we spend weekends. I like the weather at the coast. I don't like hot weather.

People complain about the fog, but I like it. They can't see the ocean so well, so we get to stay around the property, and I get more bones.

A perfect day starts about 7:00 A.M. I usually have to go pee so I nuzzle my lady, who sleepily gets out of her down comforter and staggers up (or down, depending on the house) to the door and lets me out. I don't think she opens her eyes. If we are at the coast, she puts on her robe and goes out to get the paper. Then she is awake. That usually means I get my breakfast earlier than if she goes back to bed.

Pretty often I see other dogs. If we walk in the greenbelt, there are lots of dogs being walked. There is one pit bull who thinks he's king of the path. I don't let him scare me, but I do take care to keep my lady between him and me. I never forget I'm there to protect her, but there's no sense being foolish about it.

On the coast, we used to run free in the dunes. Then the State Park got up in arms and banned dogs everywhere. I know lots of people argued that we could just be kept away from the plover. (A plover is some kind of bird they apparently think I would chase. If they would listen, I would tell them I only chase cats and squirrels. We have lots of quail walking around our property, and I can't be bothered to even notice them.) They still let the horses go on the path right behind our house, so I just sit by the fence and watch. I don't even bark anymore. Horses are pretty dumb though. Lots of time they jump when they see me, even if I don't move. I hate it when they get off the path and tear up the sand next to our house. I still wonder why the Park system thinks they don't scare the plover.

One day there was a lot of excitement. A horse came by without a rider. He was running really fast and other riders were chasing him. I never saw how it ended. I guess he ran back to his stable. I did see a woman walking down the path later, and she looked pretty mad. Maybe she wasn't a very good rider. Sometimes people do take their dogs to the beach. This really makes my lady mad, since she tries to follow the rules, even the ones that don't make sense. One lady brings her big dog (it looks like she may have some Australian cattle dog in her and maybe some greyhound.) The dog hates me. We see each other at meetings sometimes and she growls and snaps at me. She is really big so I snap back but always know how to retreat if necessary. Anyhow, they let her run to the beach, not even on a leash. I really wish I could go but I wouldn't want to be with her.

There are some beaches I can go to. I go to a little beach (where the only waves are from the tide) whenever the grandkids come to visit. I really like to run in the sand, but I am *not* a water dog. The only water I like is in my bowl (or in the toilet if I can sneak in). I don't like to swim and when I fell into our swimming pool one day, I was really scared. I think sheepdogs did not invent the dog paddle.

There is one really big beach with big waves and lots of shells. I think they even call it Shell Beach. It's fun to go to but the beach is covered with little stones, and it's not as much fun to run in as the sand behind our house. People come to park above that beach and watch the big waves. Some even stay there until it's almost dark, watching the big sun go down and the ocean turn dark. When that happens, I just want to be in my warm kitchen getting my supper. I go to bed soon after it gets dark, and I don't want to be out where the waves are crashing and the mist makes my fur all wet. I like my big warm sheepskin-covered bed.

Fifteen

I get a little tired of riding back and forth from the coast to the office. Sometimes I go in David's truck. That gives me a lot of room to walk around but usually it means that my lady isn't there. When I ride with her, she puts up a canvas lining to let me lie down but not roam around like I can in the truck. The only time that gets tricky is if one of the grandkids sits in the back seat with me and then the canvas comes down. I guess life is full of tradeoffs. I like some of the grandkids a lot. Annie is really nice to me, and so is Kady. The others don't pay much attention.

I don't miss other dogs much, but I do enjoy touching noses once in awhile to see how they see the world. Sometimes I get to run free with Annie's two big Labs and that is fun. I can outrun both of them, but they are better at catching balls and stuff. Kady's big dog, Mac, is a Lab too. He is even faster than I am, but I can turn quicker. He really likes to play unless their little dog is there. He is a pain and just growls and snaps. He's some kind of fancy dog, Bichon poodle or something, but he doesn't really like to play. Mac thinks he has to protect him and sometimes that means none of us get to play. Mac tells me that the only thing he loves is his master (my lady's son) and going hunting. He tells me that he loves to swim in that cold water and bring back the ducks. He likes to get up early and go tromp through the wheat fields up in North County. Not for me.

The only thing I think I would like to try is herding some sheep. When we drive through on the way to the coast there are lots of sheep. Sometimes when there are little lambs, there are lots of sheep right by the road. My lady rolls the window down to see them, and when I smell them I get a little urge to get out and herd them. I don't know if I really could, and pretty soon other smells make me forget. I talked to one dog who was in the truck next to us at the post office in Bodega Bay. He said he didn't really get to herd them much since all the pastures were fenced. He said he had gone up to the mountains once with his master, who was from Spain, and he got to really herd the sheep. He said it was great sleeping right with his master and being outdoors. He said he got lots of thorns, though, so maybe he preferred it down here.

Sixteen

It's a funny thing, this life with humans. Just as you get used to something, they change it. I was just getting used to this life of spending two hours in the car to get to the office, from the house on the coast, and then being in the hot climate all week and then going back to the coast again. Then my lady decided to leave.

She patted and held me and told me she would be back. I didn't think much about it. I kissed her face as usual, and when she put me down I just went to the corner of the big yard where I sit and wait for her. At nighttime David brought me in. He patted me and I got to sleep by the bed where he was sleeping, just like usual. But my lady didn't come back.

I don't have a very good idea of time. I know when it's time to get up and when it's time to eat. When it gets dark I want to go to bed (night-night they call it). Sometimes I can't get my people to go to bed for a long time so I just go into the bedroom and curl up on my sheepskin-covered pillow. I always dream about running. Sometimes I talk in my sleep and my lady (if she's there) comes and pats me and tells me that I am dreaming. I don't know exactly what she means, but I usually just go back to sleep.

I started to think I wouldn't ever see my lady again. I got very sad. Then one day David put me in the truck. We drove over to the hot town where I lived most of the time; and we went to a big, noisy place. I don't really like cars much and when they leave me in the car while they go into a store or into the post office, I usually complain. They scold me and tell me to stop barking, but I am not really barking. I just remind them that I am there and they should take me too. I only bark if someone comes too close to our car.

But this was different. There were big machines that seemed to hold hundreds of people.

I was really confused. The sidewalks were crowded with more people than I had ever seen.

They were all carrying lots of stuff. I can never figure humans out. They all seem to want to go where they aren't and take everything with them. I started to get really nervous. Was I going to get lost? Was I being taken into one of those big machines?

David put the leash on me and we got out of the truck. As we walked across the busy road, I smelled something wonderful. I pulled on my leash to get closer. Then I saw her.

My lady was coming out of the building (she called it an airport) and was carrying lots of stuff too. I was in ecstasy. My lady was home. I started singing and jumping and wriggling.

David was laughing and holding on with two hands. My lady put down all the stuff she was carrying to hug and cuddle me. I was in heaven. Maybe everything would be the same again now.

Seventeen

Since my first human vacation, I have learned more about them. I still don't understand them. The only thing I think I know is that they usually come back.

One vacation was really bad. I didn't get to go and even David went too. This time they took me out into the country, close to where I was born, and left me with a whole lot of other dogs. They called this a kennel. I know my lady had taken me there beforehand so I could see the place, but I didn't think she would ever leave me there.

It wasn't a bad place. I know she made a big deal out of having an air-conditioned place for me to stay. It really gets hot in Davis, where I live most of the time. I know she took my bed and my favorite toys with her, but the day we got up really early and drove out there, I knew she was leaving without me again.

I tried to talk her out of it. I licked her feet; I sat in front of her and showed her how good I could be. It didn't work. She took me out and handed my leash over to a nice lady who patted me and took me away from my lady. She really didn't understand dogs much. She tried to get me to eat a treat (just like my lady sometimes gave me), and she apparently thought I would really take it. I kept looking back and whining for my lady to come back. She just kept walking to the car. Then she turned back and said, "I will be back. Be a good dog."

I don't know how long I lived there. It seemed like years. I tried to adjust. I did like talking to the other dogs. Some of them were big German Shepherds who worked with something they called a police department. They thought they were better than any of the rest of us. I told them that I worked in a law office, and they treated me better after that. I don't really understand why but when I told them my lady worked in something called a court they seemed to know what I was talking about. I did meet one nice Lab. He reminded me of the one my lady's daughter has, and they are pretty easy to get along with. They are big, but I can always outrun them when we romp in the big backyard.

It seemed like forever, but one day my lady came back. She hugged and patted me, and I ran as fast as I could to jump into the back seat of her car. I made up my mind to be the best dog ever so she wouldn't go away again and leave me.

When we got to the office, all the secretaries made a fuss over me, hugged me, and said they were glad to have me back. I wasn't so sure about that because they seemed so busy and immediately started telling my lady about this and that and when I just sat down and watched, they totally ignored me. I was glad to go back to my office and under the desk. My water dish was still there, and my lady had put a treat on the floor. I am almost suspicious about those treats though. Usually when I get one, she is going to leave. The good thing about the office, though, is that she usually doesn't stay long, and I get to stay there and take care of the secretaries.

Eighteen

Like I said before, a couple of times I had to take matters into my own paws and get to the office even when my lady expected me to stay in the yard and get some fresh air. One day I figured how to open the front patio gate by putting my paw on the bottom rung and jumping up and down. When it opened, I headed for the greenbelt, which led to the office. As I ran there, I saw lots of people with dogs on leashes, but I had a mission. I was going to the office.

I figured out how to get to the real big, busy street. I was scared, but I knew I had to get across it to get to the office. I waited until a big truck went by and then dashed across the street. I followed the sidewalk. I was sure I could find the office. I went past lots of big buildings and ran on to the sidewalk to avoid the cars. Finally I found the building.

The doors were all closed. I didn't know what to do. I couldn't find my lady's car. I ran all around the building. Finally I found a window and went up to it. I saw Liz, my lady's secretary, in there working. I sat there and looked in. Then I ran around to the other window.

Pretty soon, someone opened the door to the office, and I ran in. I ran back to the door of my lady's office and sat there. The secretaries patted me and made a fuss over me. You would have thought I had done something wonderful. My lady, though, scolded me. She told me I was supposed to stay home and take care of the house, but she was really just talking while she cuddled me. I think I scared her. To tell the truth, I was a little scared too.

Each time I try this, I get scolded but patted later. I wonder if I am just looking for a little attention. I think that I am just trying to get to where my lady is, but I really know that she will come back and it would be better if I tried harder just to obey.

I keep trying to remember, but sometimes I just act and then remember later.

Nineteen

It was just like I said though. When you just get used to something, humans change it.

I was used to our big house in Davis with the swimming pool and the big yard. I knew the yippy dog behind us, and we each made sure the other didn't stray into the other's territory. I liked the little Boston terrier next door, Missy, and we used to play together on the front lawn.

Then David and my lady decided to move. It was a crazy time. Everything was pulled out and put into boxes. People came and took away our furniture. I barked and tried to protect the house but my lady just kept telling me not to bark and to stay in the back. I couldn't figure it out. Why were they taking our things?

And then our big house was empty. One day my lady put me into the car and we went to another house. It was really little. It is still in the same city, but this is a house with no yard and only a cement back patio for me to walk in. The only good thing is that the bedroom has a nice cool floor and my bed is still there right beside my lady's bed. I feel confused in this new house. It is right near the street and next door to a big building they call a church. I try to greet everyone who comes there on Wednesday night, but most often I get shut into the house. Fortunately the kitchen has a window right on the street, and I can stand up on my hind legs and watch everyone go by and be sure they don't come into my yard.

I still go to the law office. I still get to keep the secretaries busy and happy. I now get to walk to a big park near our new house and see lots of dogs and children. There are people selling stuff and I get to watch, but they won't let me walk into where they are buying food. It's great, though, when they sit down to eat and watch the grandkids play in the sprouting water fountains; they let me go under the table and eat all the meat from the overfilled sandwiches they buy from the Buckhorn. The grandkids make a big deal of the Farmers' Market and try to get me to walk with them, but I go with my lady. I don't like to have other people try to get me to walk with them.

Twenty

Now we are into a bit of a routine. We live in the little house during the week. I get to go to the office nearly every day, since there is no real yard for me to stay in. I like the little house now, since I can see out the window. It's real different. We are right downtown. There are lots of people going by our house. We go for walks and pass the fire station, the park and lots of stores. I liked our big house better, but since my lady wants to spend more time on the coast, this house suits her.

We have had a hard time getting used to the little house. It was supposed to be safe and we could leave it and safely return. That turned out not to be exactly true. One day there was a phone call to our house on the coast from the police. I wasn't exactly sure what police were, but whatever they were, they sure got my lady upset. She raced around, and although we never leave the coast on Sunday, she literally dragged me into the car and raced back toward Davis. She talked on the phone to her daughter, and asked if there was much damage. Apparently someone had broken into our house and taken many of my lady's beautiful things. I wish I had been there to protect my house.

We raced across the countryside, making me more and more uneasy. When we got to Davis, I was really scared about what was going to happen. When we raced through the city streets like they were the country roads around the coast, I was really worried. When my lady screeched into the driveway by the little house (we call it the cottage), she slammed out of the door, leaving me in the car. I was really unhappy about that. I needed to be with her to protect her from whatever was upsetting her so much. I cried to be let out. She knew I was upset, since I didn't bark in my usual shrill way when I just wanted to be let out. She ran into the house. Soon she came out and got me. I walked very close to her. I was scared. She was really upset.

When we got into the cottage, I could see why. The drawers of the desk were thrown out. There was paper and boxes all over the floor. We went downstairs. I held back. I wanted to protect her but there was a bad smell in the downstairs. I didn't know what was down there. I tried to get her not to go down, but she charged down.

It was a mess. There were things all over the floor. The bedding had been torn up; the drawers were all emptied all over the floor. Boxes were everywhere. The window had been broken into and was standing open. The police had already been there and there was that noxious black powder all over every window and door.

No police were there like they had been when we had the problem at the office. My lady just started swearing and crying at the same time. Her closet door was jammed open; the locked drawer where she kept her jewelry was jimmied open. It looked like someone had chipped away at the wood. I guess that's what they mean by "jimmying." Humans have strange words. I thought it was the same as the gym, where my lady went once or twice, and where the people all smell real good to me. But this was different.

All her jewelry was gone. She just started crying and searching to see if anything was left.

I didn't know what to do. I was scared. I was scared for her and I thought someone else was still in the closet. I whimpered and tried to get my lady to leave. She refused and just started looking under the bed and in the bathroom. Apparently there wasn't anyone still there, but the bad smell was.

She got down on her knees and looked under the bed, since all the boxes with extra sheets stored there were pulled out. The pillows on the bed had been thrown down and pillowcases taken off. The wooden drawer at the bottom was broken like someone had been standing on it while they forced the lock open on the jewelry drawer.

I just patrolled up and down, looking for something I could to do to help. She was crying. I tried licking her hand to make her feel better, but she pulled away.

When she got down, looked under the big dresser, and opened up the hidden drawer, she really broke down and cried. Her mother's gold coin necklace and that of her much-loved mother-in-law had been stolen. She started sobbing. She said that she had just moved those into the truly hidden drawer last week, to protect them—since both mothers had just died.

I couldn't console her. The man who built the house came in. I barked. I wasn't sure if he was the one who hurt my lady so much, but she quieted me and told he that he was still our friend.

He was upset too. He kept asking her what he could do to help. She was crying so much she couldn't talk. I kept trying to make her feel better. She didn't want my kisses, and I couldn't do anything else. I didn't want to stay in that mess. I went upstairs and guarded the stairway. I couldn't protect her from the bad people who had taken all our things, but no one was going to get down those stairs now. I guess it was just too late. My lady spent hours picking things up and washing all the bedding that had been ripped off. She made lists, talked on the phone, and cried all the time. I didn't know what to do.

Twenty-one

Like most things, this got a little better. My lady's daughter came and her son came and helped her. She really appreciated that, especially since he had given her much of the jewelry that had been stolen. I had never seen her so upset.

Cleaning and picking up, she started making lists. I don't really know what all was involved, but a hundred times she would stop working and swear, "Damn, they took that too. Fifty Afghan coins and they had to steal the one worth five hundred dollars."

I had no idea what she was talking about, but apparently humans like those metal things they put around their necks and on their fingers. For me, I would be happier if I didn't even have to wear the red leather collar they put on me, with all those tags that jingle when I walk.

Annie came over and played with me. I really didn't feel like playing, since my lady was so upset, but I guess I couldn't help much so I went down to the empty lot and we played a little.

Since the house was such a mess, we went over to Annie's house for supper. I like to go there. They live in an old house with a wonderful big yard and two dogs. I like to run and play with them and everybody seems happy there. There is a peacock that sits on the fence and screeches at me, since I chased it once. The big Labs chase me and pretend to be mad when I get by them into the house. They aren't really mad though, and I can outrun them anytime.

After supper we went back to the cottage. It was still a mess, but now the drawers were back in and the bed was made up. I still didn't want to go down into the bedroom, but after I prowled all around the corners and around the outside, I guess the bad guys didn't come back. We didn't sleep much though. My lady kept waking up and turning the lights on. I would go upstairs and walk all around the house. No one was there, just the sadness of the emptied drawers.

My lady spent a lot of time trying to get the police to go look for her things, but I guess they weren't very interested. She spent hours at her computer typing up lists and sending letters to some stores called "pawnshops." She called people and looked for her jewelry in the little pictures she gets on her screen (she calls it "going online"). I don't think she ever got anything back but things did get better. I got to go to the office every day now. It was sort of like my lady wanted me to be with her all the time now. We had some people put in some kind of alarm in the cottage, like the one I set off in the car when it is stopped in the shopping center and my lady forgets to fix before she goes into the store.

Twenty-two

My lady comes from a big family. She has a sister and two brothers and they have kids and other people around. I really don't know them much since they live a long ways away. When they come to visit, some of them are really nice to me, but others pretend but really try to push me away when I try to stay between them and my lady. Now she decided to go for a long car ride back to the house where she lived when she was a little girl. I supposed it would be about like our trip to Santa Fe. I don't really like riding in the car all that time, but I like being with my lady. We started planning the trip. David came and fixed everything like he does, and we started putting things together, folding clothes into little boxes they call suitcases. I put my favorite toy, my wolf, into my lady's suitcase on the floor, but she just laughed and took it out. She assured me that it would be safe here. I wasn't too sure, considering what had happened to her jewelry.

David and my lady started planning the trip. I guessed that it would be long, since they arranged for people to water the yard and take care of things. I got to go to the office and stay under the desk while my lady feverishly signed papers and sent letters and made calls.

Twenty-three

Then trouble again. One of the dogs at the dog park said it always comes in threes. I didn't think he knew much, but he was pretty old so maybe he did. We were at the office when the phone rang. My lady answered it, since it was over the noon hour and all the secretaries go away some where to eat, I guess.

She yelled and told her daughter that her house was on fire. My lady's daughter gasped. She ran out the door, leaving people in the waiting room who had come there to see her. My lady took over and set up other appointments and then we ran for the car. I knew she was upset, but I had no idea why or how upset she was.

We raced toward the house. There were police cars all over the street blocking the road.

One of the police officers came toward us and told the others to let us through because my lady was Alekka's mother.

There was a bad smell of smoke in the air. There were loud noises and many trucks lined up with hoses pouring out water. I had never seen anything like it.

Suddenly my lady pushed me into the car and took off. She realized that Annie would be coming from school and she didn't want her to hear about the fire. We rushed off to school.

Annie was still in her classroom. My lady stopped by the office and the head lady (they call her the principal) ran with us to go get Annie. Annie didn't seem upset, but she didn't know what was happening or how her life would change. I didn't really know, but I knew that my lady was really upset. When Annie told her that she had seen the fire trucks go by but they had been told that it was just a grass fire, tears started rolling down my lady's face. I tried to lick them off, but she just buckled Annie in, put me in the other corner of the back seat, and took off for the house.

The trucks were all still there. The air smelled terrible. There was smoke everywhere and everyone was just standing, looking like something terrible was happening. It was.

Annie's dad was just sitting on the grass by David. He just kept saying that it was all gone. He said they had saved nothing.

When Annie asked about her kitten, the fireman heard her and said he would try to go in and see about Luna (the kitten.) Annie was crying and smoke was rolling. Pretty soon the fireman came out with the kitten's body wrapped in a towel. Annie was really crying now. I was sad to see her so unhappy. I never really liked the kitten because it would, after all, grow up to be a cat, and when I came over they would hold my collar like I would chase it or something, but I surely didn't like to see Annie or her mother so upset. I crawled under my lady's feet, under the bench by the lawn, and watched as my lady held the kitten's body so Annie could go dig a hole to put the kitten in. Even I was sad then. When Annie's sister and brother came home, they said some magic words and put the kitten into the hole. When they put the dirt over it everybody cried. I didn't know what to do so I just licked Annie's hand and curled up under her feet.

We left pretty soon after. The big trucks started going away. My lady asked her family to come to her house, but they wanted to go with their friends. We don't have a very big house and there wouldn't be much room for all of them. We went back to our house and everyone was very quiet. My lady and David talked about the fire and tried to think of something to do for the family who had lost everything. At least they still had their dogs. The dogs had pushed out through the dog door when the fire started. Only the kitten hid (and died).

Things were pretty sad at the office after this. People kept coming by to see if they could help. I had to greet lots of new people, most of whom patted me hoping that we couldn't see them cry. Humans are funny that way. When I am sad, or hurt, I don't mind if everybody knows it. I usually get some extra treats or pats. But humans don't seem to be like that.

One little girl came by with a big sack of clothes for Annie. She had seen Annie's picture on the front page of the newspaper (taken when she found out that Luna, her kitten, was dead). She said she didn't go to the same school or know Annie, but she wanted her to have some clothes to wear to school. I guess dogs are lucky that way. We don't need to worry about what we wear, but my lady said this was a really nice thing the little girl did. She told the mother she was doing a good job!

Twenty-four

These were sad days. My family had planned this trip back to Kansas, so they decided to go ahead and go. Every year my lady apparently goes back to be in her mother's house and meet with her brothers and sisters. I don't really understand it, since I don't even remember my mother. Apparently humans do some things for their mothers after they are dead. I know they talked about flowers and stuff. It makes no sense to me, but I am just happy that they are not leaving me behind this time.

We took my lady's car and started driving. It felt a lot like the first long car trip I had been on, and it was some of the same places. We went through Oregon and stopped at Klamath Falls. The motel was not very nice but it did smell good. The young men who lived in the rooms next to ours cooked their food outside. I think they worked on ranches. There were sure a lot of them, and they spoke some other language, but they smiled a lot and smelled good to me. I don't know how early they left, though, since the big truck they all crowded into had a canvas cover over it. I know it was still dark, but my family got up pretty early too, since we had a long trip to Idaho. I always wonder about people we meet on our trips. I hope some of these young boys get to have their own dogs, since they really wanted to play with me. I disappointed them since I don't run after balls, but I did sit down and watch them eat and they seemed happy to have me there. They offered me some of the meat they were cooking, but I don't eat much of anything that my lady doesn't fix for me. They seemed surprised.

They left real early, but so did we. We had a long drive to Idaho, I guess. My lady had fixed a picnic basket, and we stopped for lunch every day. I got to see lots of green lawns, and I know to watch for where the big trucks all turn in. I usually have to pee real bad, but my lady sometimes makes me wait while she goes into a special room where the women run into when their cars stop. I always get my turn, though, and usually I have to go off to one side. It makes no sense to me, when that green lawn looks so soft and inviting, but I get dragged off to the side where there are rocks or chips. Pet area, they call it.

I like picnics, though, since I get to be right under the table where my family is eating. We stopped by one really big river and I watched the water going over some kind of dam. It started raining so we packed up and left, but trip along the river was interesting. I thought about learning to chase the ducks I saw, but then I remembered that I really didn't like to be wet.

Twenty-five

After a long day, we were back in Idaho. I remembered the motel. It was LaQuinta again and the same room we had been in three years before. I liked that. This time I didn't have to be in any crate and I knew the way to the back door and on to the grass. This place let me walk all around and we took lots of walks around the motel. There was the same restaurant where they let me go and eat outside. It was called some Irish name, like O'Sheas, and the girls were really nice to me. I don't really like table food, but I don't object if my lady saves some of her meat for me and shares. This time there were other people with their dogs too. It is a real friendly place. We didn't eat out at the lake this time. We had to go to lawyers' offices. I think lawyers are usually pretty nice. They let people bring their dogs in, especially if they know how to behave like I do. Some people are surprised when they find out that I spend my days in a law office.

Pretty soon we did go out to the lake. I like running around out there. This time I found a rabbit, but it wasn't really summer yet and the ground was still pretty cold. I guess Idaho doesn't get warm as soon as California does. It's really different from California, even at the coast. There are tall trees and the ground is covered with bushes. It has lots of rocks and there is water coming from a spring. The lake is really pretty but as I have said, I am *not* a water dog and I don't intend to go swimming or even in a boat if I can help it.

When we got ready to leave, my lady got the blankets out and put them close by the back seat. I guess it was going to be even colder where we were going. We went up north and around an even bigger lake and saw lots of little towns. I don't really understand why humans want to live around water when there are all those wonderful hills covered with trees and deer and rabbits. We even saw some sheep, but they were too far away for me to get too excited.

I made a little nest for myself and started dreaming about sheep and warm valleys.

Twenty-six

When we left Idaho, it got even colder. We went to Montana where there was a real flood. We didn't get wet but when we saw all the rivers running over their banks, I got a little scared. In one place, after we tried to drive up to Glacier National Park, the water was right at the road, and I thought we should leave right away. My lady agreed with me, and we went another road. There was snow there. I remembered that feeling from my earlier trip to Arizona. My feet get very cold. This time, though, it didn't snow on us while we were driving until we got to South Dakota.

The Park was full of mountains with lots of snow on them. We tried to drive up the narrow roads even though the Rangers in the little Park village and the people who worked there had been sure we wouldn't get through. We didn't.

I got to see some other Indians here. They were nice to me too. I had to stay outside while my family went into the stores and one man came up to talk to me in the car. I didn't even bark because he knew how to talk to dogs. He smelled a little like sheep too, so I felt happy to see him. He didn't look like the people in New Mexico or the Navajos, but I heard my lady saying that she was buying her grandkids books about the Plains Indians so they could learn about the first people who had lived here. One man outside said to a tourist that he was a Sioux. I thought he was talking about law, but apparently that is the name of a big group called a tribe.

The girls in the shop waved goodbye to me when they walked by the car as I waited. I wonder why people in cities can't be so nice or smell so good?

There was a lot of car time going across Montana. It's a pretty big place but I loved it.

Sitting in the backseat, looking out the window, I could see the sky, the hills, the mountains, and the trees. Not being one especially interested in any of the former, I was eager to get out when I saw the deer, the rabbits, and the squirrels. It wasn't going to happen even though I would nudge whoever was driving once in awhile and they would just tell me that I had just been out and to lie down. Sometimes they just don't understand me.

But when we got to Kalispell, the hotel was warm and welcoming. I quickly found the back door that led to the morning point (where I went to pee), and I enjoyed the dog biscuit the manager gave me as we checked in. My lady was eager to get to the indoor pool, but that was off limits to me, so I just lay down to catch some zzz's. Then the best luck happened. My lady got out the phone book and started calling restaurants. She found a wonderful barbecue, out on the frontage of the mountains, looking up at the road to Glacier National Park. The manager said they had never been asked, but they saw no reason why one could not bring their dog to the outside patio. It was wonderful. My family loved the food; the view was spectacular. We got lost getting there, but the beauty of cell phones came through again. People who had not worked more than a few hours guided us.

That was interesting to me. In this part of the world, the people who waited on you were summer help. The summer had just started (it was late May) and they didn't know much yet.

To cover their lack of information, they always patted me and if they could, offered me a dog biscuit. It helped them cover an embarrassment of their lack of information, and I loved it.

We stayed in Kalispell two nights. That was enough time to discover the huckleberry ice cream and have me spend a lot of time in the car while my lady shopped in the National Park book store. I know she has a lot of grandkids, but she could shop a little faster and not just load us down with books about the Native Americans who lived in the area. Maybe I'm just jealous because there are no books for dogs. Maybe I could get my lady to start books on tape for dogs.

We loved it here, but then we had to move on. We left early to drive across Montana to Billings. We stopped at the rest stop for lunch, but the pet area was quite unimpressive and the signs were stated firmly that pets were not to step on the grass. My family follows signs, but the Paths led to a nice table, and I got to spend the lunchtime comfortably surrounded by the grass lawn (but not *on* it.)

In Billings, we could find only a Best Western motel that allowed dogs (for a deposit). It was nice, with a door directly to the room. I was tired and quickly curled up to sleep. My lady went to take a swim, only to discover that the pool was only three feet deep and quickly became a playground for kids who wanted to make noise and swing on hanging balls. She wasn't very happy but perked up when we were told that the best hotel in town had a wonderful restaurant. She called and discovered that they had an outdoor patio and although no one had ever asked, the manager said "why not".

He said we could come to the Rex and just come into the patio and I could be under the table. My family warned me to be on my best behavior, and we drove into the downtown of the city and found the hotel. People smiled at me and when I just went under the table like I do under the desk at the office, the waitress was pleased, and we got good service.

When we took off the next day, I kept hearing my family talk about Custer and a war or something. It didn't mean anything to me, but they drove way up to someplace that celebrated the Battle of the Little Big Horn. I didn't know what horn they were talking about (not being very musical), but they seemed very intent in finding out how the battle had happened. Like most national parks, I had to stay in the car. I didn't like that very much, but my family didn't stay inside very long. True to form my lady bought a bunch of books and cluttered up my seat, but she seemed very interested in the Indians' abilities. I went with them as they drove up and looked around where the battle had happened, but it didn't really look like much. I didn't see how Indians could have ambushed the Army in that territory. I didn't see any trees or big hills to hide behind.

They talked about Indians for most of the morning. We drove through the Crow reservation, and it looked pretty quiet. There didn't seem to be much going on, and I hoped that the families who lived there had enough to eat. I sort of lost interest because I couldn't even see a rabbit or a deer so I just went to sleep. It looked a little sad.

The road that day was long. We detoured into Butte, since my lady wanted to see the old Anaconda mine. It was pretty high and my ears hurt, but I tried not to complain. It looked like a bunch of old buildings and the streets were very narrow. When they stopped to take pictures of the old mine, I knew enough to stay low and not even ask to go out. It didn't look like a good territory for a dog.

When we went to Bozeman the air seemed thin and I couldn't sleep. It was okay though, since I was looking out the window. I saw a deer that wasn't a deer. They said it was an antelope, but I couldn't get out to chase it. (I still pride myself on catching a deer at our house in Bodega Bay, but I quickly learned that they really kick and that you don't want to hold on to one. I think they have me figured out now, since they live in the copse of trees just behind our house.)

The only sadness this day was my lady saying over and over that she wished she could re-visit Yellowstone. I don't know what this is, but she said she had worked there at a place called Old Faithful and really wanted to see it. It was not to be. I couldn't really understand this since I don't think lawyers work out in this country, but my lady kept talking about being a manager of a soda fountain and having a bear walk her home every night. I was glad we weren't going there because I am not sure I could stand having a bear near my lady. I think bears are a lot bigger than I am and probably a lot stronger too. I would do my best, but I was glad I didn't have to test myself like that.

When we got to South Dakota it was raining. It was *really* raining. We couldn't find the hotel, and we drove around and around. We finally found the AmeriInn behind several other motels, and we moved in. It was really nice, after an initial fuss about having me come into the room without a charge. My lady had the paper from the computer that showed what the bill was supposed to be, they finally agreed, and we got a great room. It had a Jacuzzi bathtub right in the room, and I could just lie there out of harm's way and watch my family relax. They didn't have to go to the pool (although my lady did), and they could just stay where I could watch them. I wish more motels were built like that.

The next day my family set out to see some mountain called Mount Rushmore. I just wanted to stay in the nice, warm room, but I wanted to go with them even more. They started out and I couldn't see anything. I mean, *anything*. We couldn't see the road; we couldn't see the mountain; we couldn't see the other cars. We were in the middle of a cloud. It was snowing/sleeting but we could deal with that. This was oblivion. I had *never* been that close to a cloud before.

After a fair amount of swearing and yelling, my lady drove into the Mount Rushmore parking lot. It was raining and there were no signs. Dutifully putting me on my leash, she started up the mountain to see the carvings. I didn't know what we were doing there since I couldn't even see the mountain let alone any carvings. A ranger came out and asked if I was a Special Dog.

I was a little insulted when my lady said no, and he told her that I couldn't go even on the rock path unless I was in that "special" group.

David took me back to the car. I spent the morning dry and warm. For once, I was glad to stay in the car and let them slog through the rain and try to see what they had come to see. They never did. Apparently they saw a lot of pictures and learned a lot, but came out very frustrated about not seeing the sculptures. They had found another mountain to see: the carvings of Crazy Horse. I couldn't imagine going to see a sculpture of a horse, but I found out that my lady was still on the Indian trail and that Crazy Horse was an important leader.

After more traveling through the cloud, the light came through and we could see the carving on the mountain. My family left me in the car and went inside the museum to see the Indian art and find out about the carving. They were happy when they came back. That was a good thing, since the trip back down the mountain was still in the cloud, and we couldn't see even the sides of the road.

Back in Rapid City, my family went to dinner, leaving me in the car. They found a nice restaurant, The Minerva, and braved pouring rain to go eat. It was the day of a political event. They talked about sitting by a state senator who was going to run for governor of South Dakota, and my lady was very happy about the fact that the people next to her had been walking precincts for Hillary Clinton and were sure she would win in the election the next day. I had walked some precincts back in Davis with my lady, and I knew it was hard work. I was glad we didn't have to do it in South Dakota (especially in the rain.)

The weather the next day was terrible. We were going to drive to Kansas, through Nebraska. It was snowing; sleeting, hailing, and raining, and the wind was blowing like crazy.

Ever since we had been in South Dakota, we had been hearing about tornadoes. It was on the television that there were warnings where we were and where we were going to be. My lady just laughed. She said when you grow up in Kansas, you just accept tornadoes as a part of life. I don't think I could do that. I am not entirely sure what a tornado is, but when I saw the pictures on the television and saw people flying through the air, I didn't want to see one first hand. I will stay with my threat of earthquakes in California, thank you.

The drive was very scary. It took a lot of time to cross Nebraska because the weather was so bad. On one road we started out in the rain, then it hailed and strong winds pushed our car around on the road. The radio kept telling my family that a tornado had just been sighted near where we were. They wouldn't stop. I didn't even tell them when I had to pee because I didn't want to get out of the car.

I was glad when we got to Kearney. They got out for a bit. I was real quick about my business, got right back into the car, and stayed there until they stopped for groceries in Alma.

When we crossed a big dam, my lady said we were in Kansas, where she was born.

Twenty-seven

We finally got to Kansas, and we went to the house where my lady grew up. This was a special place for me, but it wasn't really very big. We met her brothers and sister and I got to sleep in the room where my lady slept when she was a little girl. It was okay with me as long as I got to be near her.

The wind was really blowing and the big tree outside her bedroom moaned with each blast. She didn't seem scared, but I was worried. When the lightning cracked and the thunder roared, like it was just outside our window, I whimpered. I was homesick for California where we don't have those kind of storms (or at least we hadn't in my lifetime.)

They were still saying there was going to be a tornado. My lady just laughed and went to bed. When the sheriff called early in the morning asking for caution against flooding, she just went back to sleep. I didn't know how I could help, so I went back to sleep too.

Being in a household where there are grown up brothers and sisters is a very interesting experience. I never saw my own after we left the kennel. I had no experience with this. One brother talked to me (he said he missed his own dog) but didn't really want me around. Another brother sort of ignored me but was kind to me whenever the occasion arose. That was okay by me. Since my lady did most of the cooking, I just hung out in the corner of the kitchen. That worked out all right.

The sister was the most interested in me. She had a dog, and she knew how to talk to me. She included me in but never really realized that I only wanted to be by my lady, no matter who all was in the room. It was all okay though except when they went to church, and I was left in the car. I yipped, like I do at the post office or the gas station, and one brother got really upset. He said some cross things to my lady, and she got upset too. I stayed away from him after that.

Twenty-eight

The rest of the family left a day before my family did. That extra day was nice. We walked around the cornfield and looked at the crops. I think they were corn and soybeans, but I couldn't find any beans to eat. I got to chase a squirrel and then a rabbit. I got to run free for a time and that was great. Maybe I could get to like Kansas, except for the thunder and lightning. That had scared me. There were some different customs too.

The family had all gone to a place they called a graveyard. They took bunches of flowers and decorated the lumps of earth they called graves. I didn't really understand but they seemed very upset by being there and some of them cried. I guess my lady's mother and father were buried there, and she wanted to think about them. I never knew my father and I haven't seen my mother since I was lucky enough to be with my lady. I wouldn't care about them, but I guess I would be sad if it were my lady under the ground. Dogs don't think about things like this, but we don't like to see our people sad. I don't think that land really had their family there, but maybe it was just thinking about them that made them remember. I am more interested in what is happening today, but maybe that is the difference between dogs and humans.

Twenty-nine

When we left Kansas, we drove to Colorado. It was an easy drive compared to the ones we had been on. We went to visit some friends of my lady. Anina and Terry are really nice people. They invited me into their house and made me feel at home. They never said not to do anything, and they made sure that I had water to drink and food to eat. I liked them, and I was sad when we had to leave. Denver is a big city, and we drove around. I was okay to stay in the house by myself, which is really unusual for me. That's what happens when the people you stay with are really nice to you. I took care of their house just like it was mine.

When we left Denver, we went back into the snow country. We drove through high mountains and watched the streams fall down the sides of the hill. I liked that. It makes a nice sound when the water comes down the side of the mountain. It wasn't too cold, either. We stopped a few times but drove on to Utah. We had another LaQuinta in Moab and I knew what to expect in the motel. We didn't have much water around though. It was dry and a little dusty. I think this is what they call another desert. I don't think I would like it in the summertime. I got pretty hot even though it was late May. We drove up to see some red rocks they called the Arches. David took lots of pictures. I don't think my lady was too excited about it, but she drove all around so he could see whatever he wanted. To me, they all looked pretty much alike. I never saw any deer or antelope—not even a rabbit. We left there and drove down to see a Hole in the Wall, which was where someone dug a house inside the mountain. I couldn't go in and David didn't want to, so we waited while my lady went in to see the house built under the mountain. I don't think she was very impressed. We then went to a wonderful rest stop and sat at the foot of another mountain while the breeze blew through. That was nice.

Thirty

I was ready to go home. I think my family was too. We had decided not to go down to Mesa Verde, since David got to see the display at the museum in Denver and my lady had already been there. So we just took off going west. My lady had made a reservation in Wendover, Nevada, not realizing that we could drive so quickly around Salt Lake, but they wouldn't let her cancel it so we stopped early. That was okay with me. I don't really like the desert, and this wasn't a very nice place. David and I took a long nap and my lady went out exploring. There wasn't much to see: some rundown casinos plus a fancy one that none of us wanted to go into (as if they would have let me in). I stayed in the car while they ate in one…and brought their steak back to me. It wasn't very good!

My lady and I walked out into the desert. It is a very lonely-looking place. I was glad when we left and started the long drive back to California. We had planned to stop in Reno but couldn't do it. There was no way my lady was going to stop two hours from home when we have such a nice house to go to. We pushed on through. I was very glad to see the causeway and the long approach to Davis. I'm not a duck dog, like Mac, but the sight of hundreds of ducks flying is very exciting.

I was glad to know that in just a little more time I could be out of the car and back in my own backyard. I was glad to go to the office the next morning and then back to the coast, where I really love it. I am still tired, but it is cool and the sand feels good under my feet.

Thirty-one

I thought we had traveled enough but this summer we started off again. This time I pretty much knew what to expect, and they didn't bother taking any crates or anything. I was glad to see that they took my big round bed sheepskin-covered bed, which I love. I had the backseat all to myself, and I could look out at the mountains. It seems like every time we go somewhere, we start by going through mountains and my ears always hurt.

It didn't last long this time, but I knew we were up high. The mountains were tall but dry. David said these were the Eastern Sierras, where he was born.

We went down near another lake called Mammoth (although I never saw a lake called that—just a mountain) and stayed at a place called Convict Lake. It was a really little cabin, but I liked it because my family was never out of sight. I could lie on the porch and watch all the other dogs who were there with their families. One little dog looked like a rat. He belonged to the man who cleaned our cabin, and the little dog thought the cabin was his. I soon set him straight. He was so little though that I just had to growl and he backed away. When the Rottweiler came on to our deck, that was a different story. I backed into our doorway and barked as loud as I could. My lady came out and yelled at him; his owner came and apologized.

We took long dusty hikes into the mountains. My lady said some of the trees were more than 4,000 years old. I didn't really want to see any more bristlecone pines, but my lady was really impressed. She kept saying that these trees were here before people. The ground was white and hot, and I couldn't see why people ever came here. This was *not* like the white ground at Flagstaff. We didn't stay long but drove down a long road to Bishop.

David was born in a fish hatchery. We spent a lot of time walking around long tanks of fish. They called it Hot Creek Fish Hatchery, and the people were really nice, but one fish pretty much looks like any other to me. I did like the smell of the food they fed the baby fish. It smelled a little like the chips I eat. Anyway, we went to another hatchery that was being built, and the people there were really nice. David was happy; I was happy when we turned for home.

I have a feeling we'll be back here since David was so happy here. But now, we are going back where I sort of know what to expect. I miss my office—and the sand dunes of the coast.

Thirty-two

After a long trip home, the office was really busy but otherwise seemed the same. The secretaries are glad to see me, and the office is cool. After I checked on all the babies and found that Nicholas (Teresa's baby) was now almost as big as Miles, I resigned as babysitter. After a little time we got back into the car and went to the coast where the weather is cool and foggy (it's summer, after all).

I think I'll sign off now. Maybe pretty soon we won't be in Davis much except to visit. Maybe soon my lady won't be at the law office except once in awhile. Maybe soon the big desk that has provided my den for these many years will belong to someone else. That will be okay as long as I am with my lady. We can spend more time on the coast, and I can keep trying to convince those deer who think our yard is their dinner that I am going to catch them (*not!*). I keep trying to help my lady learn how to do the move she calls "downward facing dog". I don't know why it's so hard for her. I do it fifty times a day. I keep telling her *not* to put her head down! Oh well.

I won't have any puppies to tell this to, but I talk to my friends when we walk and to the Labs when we go visit. They're jealous because their people don't take them to their law offices. So I'll enjoy what I have before my humans change. If they go on any more car trips, I just hope they take me along. That and my food at 7:00 and 5:00 are all I ask. Life is good. Enjoy!